TRAINS

CHRIS OXLADE

A⁺

Smart Apple Media

Published by Smart Apple Media
2140 Howard Drive West, North Mankato, Minnesota 56003

Created by Q2A Creative, Editor: Chester Fisher, Designers: Amandeep K. Bakshi, Ashita Murgai
Picture Researcher: Lalit Dalal, Somnath Bowmick

Picture Credits
Albert Jeans: 14b, Alstom: 16 & 17t, Bridgnorth cliff railway: 25t, Chris Barton: 5b,
Ffestiniog Railway Co: 13b, Gregor.V/www.Parovoz.com: 9b, Hashimoto Noboru/Corbis
Sygma: 29t, Jeff Williams/Shutterstock: 8b, Orient-Express Hotels,
Trains & Cruises: 20c & 20br & 21b, Pilatus-Bahnen: 24,
Rail Photo Library: 15tr & 18b & 19t & 23b & 27t & 27b,
Rebecca Picard/Shutterstock: 5t, Science and Society
Picture Library: 10t & 10-11cb, Siemens AG: 4b, 6b, 7t, 9cl,
14t, 17b, 22cr, 22b & 26b Shutterstock: 12b & 13t,
Steamtown National Historic Site: 23t The Trans-Siberian
Express Company/GW Travel Ltd: 21t www.steamlocomotive.com: 11t & 31tr

Printed in United States

Library of Congress Cataloging-in-Publication Data
Oxlade, Chris
Trains / by Chris Oxlade
p. cm. — (Mighty machines)
Includes index.
ISBN-13: 978-1-58340-922-0
1. Railroads—Juvenile literature. I. Title. II. Series.

TF148.O95 2006
385—dc22   2006002934

P.O. 86816   10107

4 6 8 9 7 5 3

CONTENTS

MIGHTY TRAINS

Every day, thousands of trains carry millions of passengers and millions of tons of freight between towns and cities all over the world.

TYPES OF TRAINS

There are two main types of trains: passenger trains and freight trains. Passenger trains come in several different forms. High-speed trains operate nonstop between big cities. Commuter trains carry workers into cities and out again. Light rail trains run through city centers. All trains are made up of two or more rail vehicles linked together.

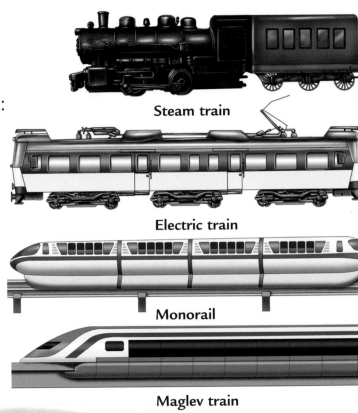

Steam train

Electric train

Monorail

Maglev train

The ICE 3 is a high-speed train that carries passengers at speeds of more than 185 miles (300 km) per hour.

TRACK AND INFRASTRUCTURE

Trains would be useless without tracks to travel on. Most tracks are made up of two metal rails supported on concrete or wooden ties. The distance between the rails is called the track gauge. Railroads also need other infrastructure, such as stations, bridges, and tunnels, as well as signals to control the trains.

A busy train station where many people arrive and depart.

FAST FACTS

Busiest Station
The world's busiest station is Shinjuku Station in Tokyo, Japan. 1.6 million passengers pass through it daily.

Railroad track stretching into the Bolivian desert. There are millions of miles of railroad tracks in the world.

ELECTRIC TRAINS

The wheels of an electric locomotive are turned by electric motors. Electric locomotives are fast, quiet, and clean.

ELECTRIC LOCOMOTIVES

A locomotive is a railroad vehicle that pulls other vehicles, such as passenger coaches or freight cars. An electric locomotive picks up electricity from an overhead cable. Electrical machinery in the locomotive changes the voltage of the electricity and controls how it flows to the electric traction motors that turn the wheels.

Transformer and rectifier
Reduces voltage and changes to direct current

Pantograph
Collects high-voltage alternating current

Siemens 1047 Eurosprinter

Power	8,582 horsepower
Weight	95 tons (86 t)
Traction motors	2
Top speed	145 miles (230 km) per hour

Truck
Contains wheels and traction motors

A modern electric locomotive that pulls freight cars in Europe.

www.dispolok.com
ES 64 F4-001
SIEMENS
www.dispolok.com
dispolok
ES 64 F4-001

In an electric multiple unit (EMU), each coach has its own traction motors. There is no separate locomotive.

TRUCKS

All modern trains have trucks. A truck is a frame with four (or sometimes six) wheels. A locomotive has two trucks, one at each end. The trucks swivel from side to side when the locomotive goes around a bend in the track. A locomotive truck has a traction motor that turns its wheels.

FAST FACTS
The Third Rail
Some electric locomotives get their electricity from an extra rail in the track called the third rail.

Traction motor

Truck frame

Wheel

The truck system on the Paris Metro.

7

DIESEL TRAINS

The power that moves a diesel train comes from a giant onboard diesel engine. Diesel locomotives can travel where there is no electric supply.

DIESEL LOCOMOTIVE

Most diesel locomotives are actually diesel-electric locomotives. This means that the diesel engine turns an electric generator. The generator makes electricity that works electric traction motors that turn the wheels. Some locomotives are diesel-mechanical locomotives, which means that the diesel engine drives the wheels by gears. Diesel-hydraulics are driven by hydraulic systems.

Locomotive number
Identifies the locomotive

Running light
White when train is moving forward at night

General Electric Genesis	
Power	4,200 horsepower
Weight	133 tons (121 t)
Traction motor	4
Top speed	110 miles (177 km) per hour

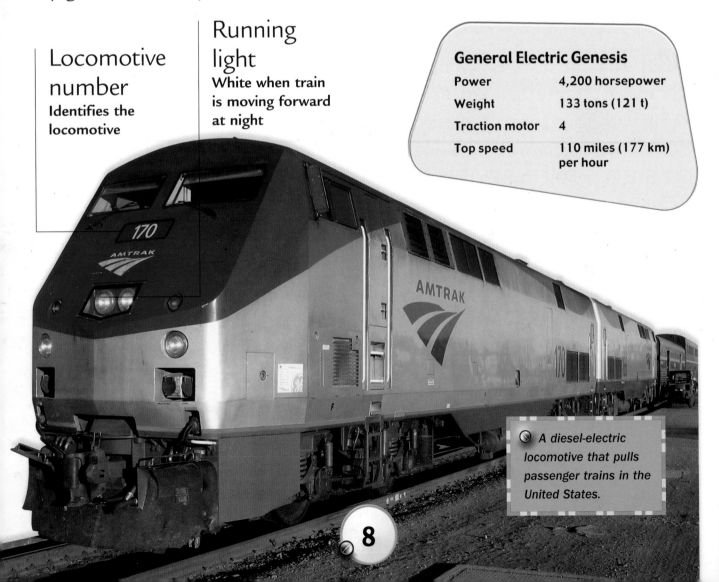

A diesel-electric locomotive that pulls passenger trains in the United States.

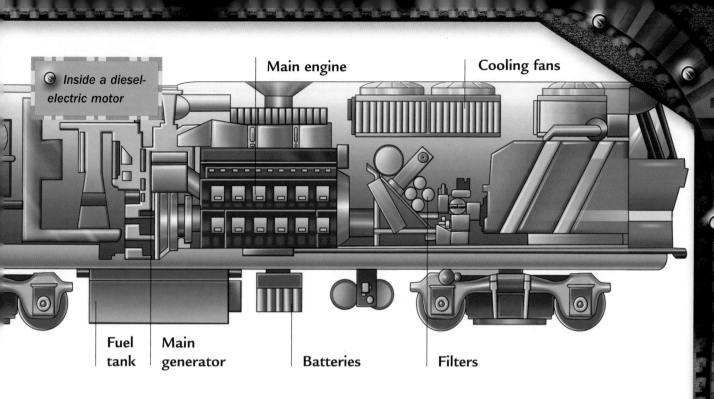

Inside a diesel-electric motor

Main engine

Cooling fans

Fuel tank | Main generator | Batteries | Filters

DIESEL POWER

The diesel engines in diesel locomotives are giant machines. The biggest weigh more than 22 tons (20 t) and have 16 cylinders and a turbocharger. Each cylinder has a capacity of more than two and a half gallons (10 l). A typical car engine with 4 cylinders only has a total capacity of about half a gallon (1.6 l).

FAST FACTS
Power Engine
The diesel engine from a diesel-electric locomotive is 50 times more powerful than a typical car engine.

The controls and instruments in the cab of a diesel locomotive.

EARLY TRAINS

The first trains worked in mines more than 250 years ago. They were small trucks pulled by people or horses. Steam locomotives were invented about 200 years ago.

Stephenson's Rocket could pull a train at 30 miles (48 km) per hour.

ROCKET POWER

The *Rocket* is one of the most famous steam locomotives. It was built by British engineer and inventor George Stephenson. It won a competition in 1830 to pull trains on one of the first railroads, between Liverpool and Manchester in Britain. Most of the locomotives built later were based on the *Rocket*.

An 1830s first-class railroad coach was luxurious, but the ride was very bumpy!

Buffer
Keeps coaches from bumping together as train slows

This is a replica of an American locomotive of the 1860s. At the front is a cowcatcher, which protected the locomotive from objects on the track.

Cowcatcher

Cylinder and piston

Driving wheels

Boiler

IMPROVING POWER AND SPEED

During the 1840s and 1850s, engineers built locomotives with bigger and bigger fireboxes and boilers, which gave more steam at higher pressure. This made the locomotives more powerful. The number of wheels driven by the pistons was increased to four or six. This kept the wheels from slipping.

FAST FACTS
Traveling in Comfort
On early railroads, wealthy passengers could load their horse-drawn carriages onto freight cars and travel inside of them in comfort.

STEAM TRAINS

Steam locomotives ruled the railroads in the first half of the 20th century. More efficient and cleaner electric and diesel locomotives took over in the 1960s.

High-pressure steam in

Valve

Piston

Exhaust-steam out

Drive rod

Cylinder

How it works

A valve lets high-pressure steam into the cylinder to push the piston and drive the wheels. The valve then lets out the exhaust steam.

STEAM POWER

The energy for a steam locomotive comes from burning coal in the firebox. The hot gases boil water to make high-pressure steam. The steam is piped to the cylinders, where it makes the pistons move in and out, making the wheels turn. A roaring, puffing steam locomotive made an impressive sight as it hurtled along the track.

An 1899 locomotive used in the American West.

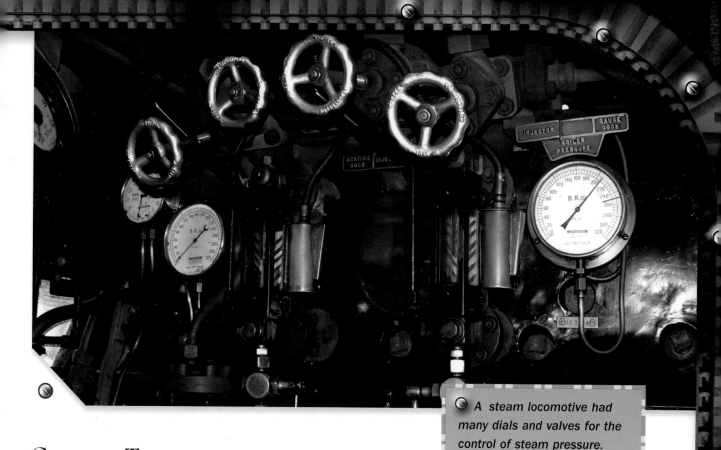

A steam locomotive had many dials and valves for the control of steam pressure.

STEAM TODAY

There are hundreds of steam locomotives still working around the world today. In some countries, such as China and India, steam locomotives still pull passenger and freight trains. There are also many preserved steam locomotives that are run by enthusiasts. They pull passenger trains on scenic railroad lines.

FAST FACTS

Fastest Steam Train
The fastest steam locomotive of all time was the Mallard. *In 1938, it set a speed record of 127 miles (203 km) per hour.*

A preserved steam engine on the Ffestiniog railroad in Wales. Originally, this railroad moved slate from mines to ships on the coast.

Saddle tank
The water tank sits over the firebox

HIGH-SPEED

Modern high-speed trains carry passengers quickly and comfortably between cities. They can travel at 185 miles (300 km) per hour on specially built high-speed tracks.

HIGH-SPEED SETS

All high-speed trains come in train "sets." Each set is made up of two streamlined end cars with high-speed coaches in between. The two end cars are normally power cars that collect electricity from overhead cables and send it to the traction motors. Nearly all high-speed trains are powered by electricity.

Inside a coach of the Spanish Velaro high-speed train.

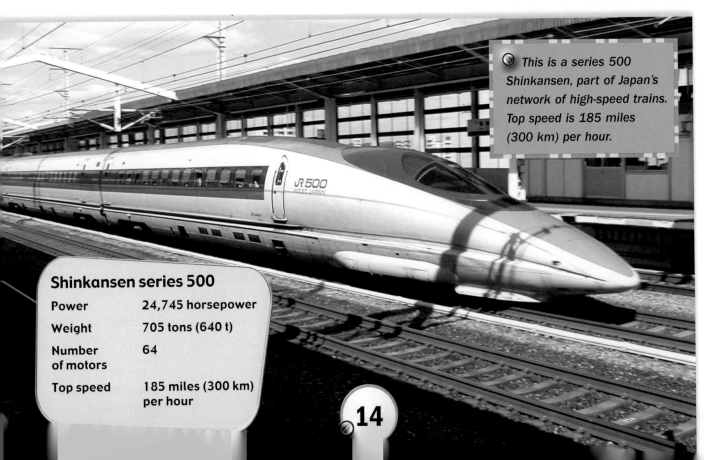

This is a series 500 Shinkansen, part of Japan's network of high-speed trains. Top speed is 185 miles (300 km) per hour.

Shinkansen series 500	
Power	24,745 horsepower
Weight	705 tons (640 t)
Number of motors	64
Top speed	185 miles (300 km) per hour

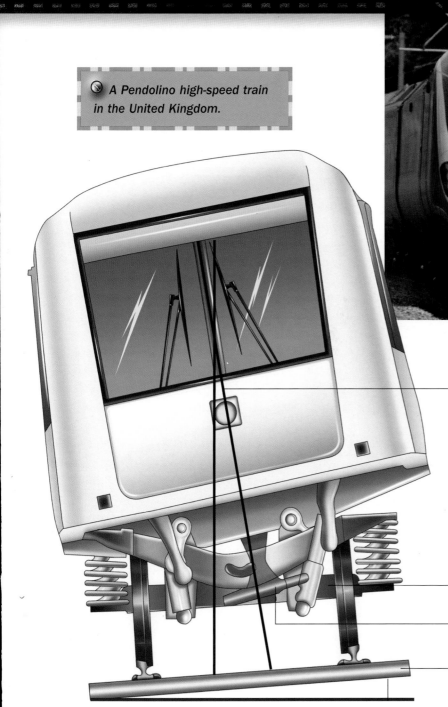

A Pendolino high-speed train in the United Kingdom.

Car body tilt angle

Tilting trains are used to overcome problems on curving railroad tracks.

Truck frame

Tilting ram

Track

TILTING TRAINS

Some high-speed trains tilt as they go around bends, just as you lean sideways as you go around a corner on a bicycle. Tilting lets the train go faster around bends than normal because it keeps passengers, luggage, cups, and other objects from flying sideways. The tilting is controlled by onboard computers.

FAST FACTS
Fastest Electric Train
The fastest speed ever reached by an electric train is 320 miles (515 km) per hour, by a TGV train in France in 1990.

MASS TRANSIT

Metro trains and light rail trains stop at stations in cities. They are designed to transport hundreds of people and are called mass transit trains.

METRO TRAINS

Metro trains are mass transit trains that run on normal railroad tracks. Metro trains have good acceleration, so they can get between stations quickly. They are normally electric multiple units or diesel multiple units. Many major cities also have subways that run through tunnels under the streets.

This is Metro System Shanghai Pearl Line in Shanghai, China.

Motor car
Two motor cars are needed for a six-car train

Standing room
Allows lots of passengers to fit into the coaches

Sliding doors
Plenty of doors so passengers can get on and off easily

A Citidas lightrail train running through the streets of Bordeaux in France.

LIGHT RAIL

Trains that run along city streets are called light rail trains. The trains are lighter than main-line trains, which means that the rails do not have to be as strong. Light rail trains often share roads with city traffic but normally have the right-of-way.

Double-decker trains carry more people than single-deckers. The floors are linked by stairs.

80-33 022-9

FREIGHT TRAINS

Thousands of different pieces of freight, from logs to light bulbs, are carried around the world by huge freight trains. Freight is carried in specialized cars.

General freight car

Oil tanker

CARS AND TANKERS

There are dozens of different types of freight cars. The simplest are boxcars and flatcars that can be packed with all sorts of freight. Some flatcars carry standard metal containers that are also carried by trucks and ships. The different cars are called rolling stock.

Flatcar
Can carry goods of all shapes and sizes

⊘ Flatcars can be adapted for special uses such as laying cable.

Containers are put on flatcars directly from ships.

Flatcar

Containers

These are standard sizes to fit most flatcars

MULTIPLE HEADERS

A long freight train, with hundreds of cars, can weigh so much that a single locomotive cannot pull it. So, two, three, or even four locomotives are coupled to each other. These trains are called multiple headers. These are often used in mountain regions where there are long, steep sections of track.

FAST FACTS

Nuclear cars

The most specialized freight cars carry nuclear fuel and nuclear waste. They are designed to survive the worst train crash.

A multiple header hauling freight through the Canadian mountains.

FAMOUS TRAINS

Some trains are famous for their luxury coaches or for the journeys they take passengers on.

Coaches of the Orient Express *were specially built by the Compagnie Internationale des Wagons-Lits.*

LUXURY COACHES

The most famous train of all was the *Orient Express*. It was the most luxurious way to travel across Europe between the 1880s and the 1940s. The coaches featured leather armchairs, fine carpets, and gold decorations. The compartments were sitting rooms by day and then converted to bedrooms at night. Food was served in the dining car.

Inside a restored coach of the modern-day Orient Express.

THE LONGEST JOURNEY

The most famous train journey in the world is that aboard the *Trans-Siberian Express*. The train runs from Moscow, across Russia, to Vladivostok on the east coast, about 5,780 miles (9,300 km) away. The trip takes 9 or 10 days, and the train stops at 91 stations on the way.

The Trans-Siberian Express running through the Russian countryside.

Celebrating 100 years of the Trans-Siberian Express.

FAST FACTS
Orient Express
The original coaches of the Orient Express have been restored and form a tourist train that is also called the Orient Express.

TRANS-SIBERIAN EXPRESS
100 Years – 100 лет
ТРАНС-СИБИРСКИЙ ЭКСПРЕСС

П36   003

RECORD BREAKERS

On these pages, you can find out about some of the world's fastest, longest, and biggest trains. They are all record breakers.

THE FASTEST

Velaro high-speed electric trains run on a specially built track between Madrid and Barcelona in Spain. They are designed to run at a top speed of 217 miles (350 km) per hour. This makes them the fastest regular trains in the world. A French TGV train holds the world record for an electric train—32 miles (515 km) per hour.

Velaro high-speed train set	
Power	11,964 horsepower
Weight	468 tons (425 t)
Number of motors	16
Top speed	217 miles (350 km) per hour

Driver's cabin
Spacious and easy to drive

Nose compartment

With a coupling mechanism

The streamlined nose of a Spanish Velaro high-speed train.

> *The biggest steam locomotives ever built were the Union Pacific Big Boys of the 1940s. One weighed a massive 605 tons (549 t).*

Piston
Powers 4 of the 16 driving wheels

FREIGHT MONSTERS

The heaviest and longest trains are mine trains that carry iron ore or coal. They are made up of hundreds of cars coupled together, with giant diesel locomotives at each end. The heaviest train ever was an Australian ore train assembled in 2001. It featured 8 locomotives and 682 cars, and was 4.5 miles (7 km) long and weighed 109,936 tons (99,732 t).

FAST FACTS
The Big Boy
Big Boy locomotives had 4 pistons that turned 16 huge driving wheels. They were 132 feet (40 m) long.

> *A mammoth Southern Pacific coal train at Tennessee Pass, Colorado.*

MOUNTAIN TRAINS

Normal trains cannot go up steep hills because their wheels slip on the track. Mountain railroads have an extra rail that the trains grip with a toothed wheel.

THE STEEPEST RAILROAD

On a rack-and-pinion railroad, the train has a cog, or pinion (a toothed wheel), that grips a rack (a toothed rail) in the center of the track. The cog is turned by the train's engine. The steepest rack railroad is the Pilatus Railroad in Switzerland. In places, the track rises up the mountainside at an incredible 48 degrees.

A train on the Pilatus Railroad. The track gains 5,344 feet (1,629 m) in 3 miles (5 km).

Stepped coach
Coach floor has different levels

Overhead cables
Supply electricity to train's motors

Cable
Pulls coach
up and lowers
it down

One of the trains on
a funicular railroad in
Bridgenorth, UK. It carries
passengers up and down
a steep hill in the town.

Frame
Keeps coach level
on steep slopes

FUNICULAR RAILROADS

Some mountain railroads have a
different traction system from the
rack-and-pinion system. They are
pulled up the mountainside by
cables. This sort of system is called
a funicular. There are normally two
tracks and two trains. As one train
goes up, the other comes down, so
they balance each other.

FAST FACTS
Jungfraubahn Railroad
*The Jungfraubahn mountain railroad
in Switzerland climbs to the top of
Jungfrau Mountain. On the way, it
climbs through a tunnel high inside
the famous Eiger Mountain.*

25

MONORAIL

A monorail is a railroad with one rail instead of the usual two. Monorail trains sit on top of the track or hang underneath it. The tracks are normally high in the air.

SUPPORTED MONORAILS

On a supported monorail, the train straddles the rail. The rail is a narrow beam. The train sits on top of the beam, and its sides hang down on each side of the beam. The track is normally held in the air on thin concrete columns. This means that the track takes up hardly any space on the ground underneath, so a monrail can be built over roads and parking lots.

The Newark International Airport monorail. The trains are powered by electric motors and run on the track on rubber tires.

Coaches
These have rubber tires which give traction and stability

Newark International Airport monorail

Length	3 miles (5 km)
Number of stations	8
Average speed	12 miles (19 km) per hour
Opened	1995

Double track
Made of steel beams and supported on steel columns

Monorail train
Moved along by electric motors

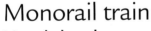

SUSPENDED MONORAILS

In some monorail systems, the coaches hang underneath the rail instead of sitting on top of it. In one type of suspended monorail, the wheels run in a channel on top of the rail. Curved arms support the coaches below. In other types, the train's wheels run along the flanges of the beam that forms the track. The flange is like a shelf that runs along the beam.

The suspended monorail in Wuppertal, Germany. The trains run above a river most of the time.

Trucks
With wheels that roll along the top of the rail

The Osaka monorail in Japan. The trains roll along the top of concrete beams. There are guide wheels on each side of the beam.

Guide wheels
Roll along each side of the track and steer the train along the track

FAST FACTS
First Monorail
The first passenger monorail opened in Britain in 1825. The train was pulled by a horse that walked along the ground.

MAGLEV TRAINS

Maglev is short for magnetic levitation. Maglev trains are the fastest trains of all. In the future, maglevs could travel as fast as jet airliners.

MAGNETIC LEVITATION

Maglev trains have no wheels. They are suspended a few inches above the track by electromagnets. This means that there is no friction between the train and the track, allowing the train to travel at very high speeds. Magnets also power the train. There are several working maglev railroads around the world.

Shanghai Transrapid maglev	
Track length	19 miles (30 km)
Journey time	8 minutes
Top speed	269 miles (430 km) per hour
Opened	2004

A Transrapid maglev train. Magnets in the track can be turned on and off to pull the train along the track.

Nose
Aerodynamic shape allows train to move smoothly at high speeds

Shanghai Transrapid

SMT

An experimental superconducting maglev train running on the Yamanashi Maglev Test Line in Japan.

SUPERCONDUCTING RAILROAD

The fastest trains in the world run on an experimental maglev railroad in Japan. They have reached speeds of 360 miles (580 km) per hour. The levitation electromagnets on the train are made of superconducting material, which must be kept extremely cold to work. The track contains propulsion electromagnets along its whole length, making it extremely expensive to build.

A front view of a Transrapid maglev train. This is a monorail maglev.

Track magnets
Produce a changing magnetic field

Onboard magnets
Attracted by the track magnets

TIMELINE

1769
In France, Nicolas Cugnot builds a steam coach, the first steam-powered vehicle.

1774
Scotsman James Watt builds a steam engine.

1789
In Britain, William Jessup invents the flanged wheel to keep railroad cars on a track.

1804
Richard Trevithick of Britain builds one of the first-ever steam locomotives.

1825
George Stephenson completes his steam locomotive, which pulls trains on the Stockton & Darlington Railway in Britain.

1830
The *Best Friend* is the first steam locomotive built in the United States. It works on the Charlston & Hamburg railroad.

1832
The *American No. 1* locomotive, with 4 driving wheels, can go 60 miles (100 km) per hour.

1833
George Stephenson invents the steam-powered brake for slowing trains.

1863
The first subway opens in London.

1869
The Central Pacific and Union Pacific meet at Promontory, Utah, linking the west and east coasts of the U.S.

1879
The first electric locomotive is demonstrated in Germany by Siemens.

1891
The *Orient Express* makes its first run from Paris to Istanbul.

1893
The first electrified railroad in the U.S. opens in Baltimore.

1897
German engineer Rudolf Diesel demonstrates his diesel engine.

1905
The Trans-Siberian Railroad is completed.

1934
The first successful diesel-electric locomotive is built.

1938
The *Mallard* sets the world speed record for a steam locomotive, marking 126 miles (203 km) per hour.

1940
The Union Pacific Big Boy locomotives are built in the U.S.

1990
In France a TGV sets the speed record for an electric train, at 320 miles (515 km) per hour.

2001
In Australia, the heaviest-ever train—109,936 tons (99,732 t)—is assembled.

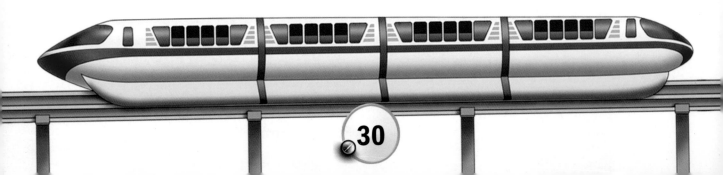

GLOSSARY

alternating current

Electric current that keeps changing direction, flowing one way and then the opposite way.

coach

A railroad vehicle for carrying passengers.

cylinder

In a steam train, part where steam from the boiler makes pistons move in and out, making the engine work.

diesel locomotive

A locomotive powered by a diesel engine.

direct current

Electric current that flows in the same direction all the time.

electric locomotive

A locomotive powered by electricity from an overhead cable or rail.

firebox

Where the fuel (coal or wood) is burned in a steam locomotive.

freight

Any goods that are carried on a train.

freight car

A railway vehicle for carrying freight.

high-voltage

Electricity with a large electric force making it flow.

iron ore

Rock that the metal iron is extracted from.

light rail

A train that runs on tracks through city streets.

locomotive

A machine that pulls railroad coaches or freight cars.

maglev

Short for magnetic levitation.

metro train

A train that carries lots of passengers and runs from city suburbs or towns into a city.

monorail

A railroad with one rail instead of two.

multiple header

A train pulled by two or more locomotives.

multiple unit

A passenger train made up of self-propelled coaches. It has no locomotive.

piston

In a steam train, the rods that are pushed in and out of cylinders by steam to drive the wheels around.

signal

A set of colored lights on a railroad that tells a train driver when to stop or keep going.

superconductor

A material that allows electricity to flow through it extremely easily.

traction motor

An electric motor that turns the wheels of a locomotive or train.

truck

A frame with 4 or 6 wheels.

valve

A device that turns on or off the flow of liquid or gas along a pipe.

INDEX

WEB FINDER

http://www.railway-technology.com *Information on the latest trains.*

http://en.wikipedia.org/wiki/Locomotive *All about different locomotives.*

http://travel.howstuffworks.com/diesel-locomotive.htm *How a diesel locomotive works.*

http://www.bbc.co.uk/history/games/rocket/rocket.shtml *Animation of Stephenson's* Rocket.

http://www.bluetrain.co.za *All about South Africa's luxury Blue Train.*

http://www.steamlocomotive.com/bigboy *Information and photographs of the biggest steam trains.*

http://www.monorails.org *All about monorail trains.*

http://www.rtri.or.jp *Site of the Japanese maglev train.*